SIMPLY SCIENCE

Solids, Liquids, Gases

by Charnan Simon

Content Adviser: Terrence E. Young Jr., M.Ed., M.L.S.,
Jefferson Parish (La.) Public Schools

Reading Adviser: Dr. Linda D. Labbo,
Department of Reading Education, College of Education,
The University of Georgia

 COMPASS POINT BOOKS

Compass Point Books
3722 West 50th Street, #115
Minneapolis, MN 55410

Visit Compass Point Books on the Internet at *www.compasspointbooks.com* or e-mail your
request to *custserv@compasspointbooks.com*

Photographs ©:

Color Box/FPG International, cover; Photo Network/Henryk T. Kaiser, cover; Visuals Unlimited/Carina Cavagnaro, cover; Karl
Weatherly/Corbis, 4; VCG/FPG International, 5; Unicorn Stock Photos/Jim Shippee, 6; Photo Network/Myrleen Cate, 7 top;
VCG/FPG International, 7 bottom; Visuals Unlimited/Nada Pecnik, 8; Duomo/Chris Trotman/Corbis, 9; David F. Clobes, 10;
Visuals Unlimited/Jeff Greenberg, 11 top; Unicorn Stock Photos/Tom McCarthy, 11 bottom; Visuals Unlimited/Jeff Greenberg,
12 top; David F. Clobes, 12 bottom; R. Pleasant/FPG International, 13; Micheal Simpson/FPG International, 14, 15; Gary Braasch/
Corbis, 16; Bettmann/Corbis, 17; David F. Clobes, 19; Unicorn Stock Photos, Jim Shippee, 20 left; Unicorn Stock Photos/
Tom McCarthy, 20 right; David F. Clobes, 21; Unicorn Stock Photos/Wayne Floyd, 23; Photo Network/Henryk T. Kaiser, 24;
Visuals Unlimited/Jeff J. Daly, 25; Carl Corey/Corbis, 27; Photo Network/David Vinyard, 28; Unicorn Stock Photos/Robert
McGinn, 29.

Editors: E. Russell Primm, Emily J. Dolbear, and Melissa Stewart
Photo Researcher: Svetlana Zhurkina
Photo Selector: Dawn Friedman
Design: Bradfordesign, Inc.

Library of Congress Cataloging-in-Publication Data

Simon, Charnan.
   Solids, liquids, gases / by Charnan Simon.
     p. cm.— (Simply science)
   Includes bibliographical references (p.) and index.
   Summary: An introduction to the properties of matter, discussing solids, liquids, and gases.
   ISBN 0-7565-0037-0 (hardcover : lib. bdg.)
     1. Matter—Properties—Juvenile literature. [1. Matter.] I. Title. II. Simply science
(Minneapolis, Minn.)
   QC173.36 .S56 2000
   530.4—dc21
                                         00-008561

Table of Contents

What Is Matter?

Think about some of your favorite things. You probably like riding your bicycle and jumping in puddles. You probably like the bubbles that tickle your nose when you drink a soda. Did you know that all these things—your bicycle, a puddle, and the bubbles in soda—are alike in one very important way? They are all made up of **matter**.

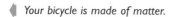
Your bicycle is made of matter.

You and rain are made of matter.

Everything in the world is made up of matter. Matter is anything that takes up space. How many different kinds of matter are there in the world? Too many to count! We can sort all matter into three main groups— **solids**, **liquids**, and **gases**.

◀ Bubbles are gases that float in liquids.

Soup is a liquid. ▶

← *The furniture in your bedroom is a solid.*

Solids

Every solid has a shape all its own. Your bicycle is a solid. It keeps its own shape when it is parked in the garage and when you are riding it on the sidewalk. Flowers and base-balls and dishes are solids too.

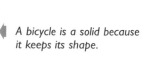

A bicycle is a solid because it keeps its shape.

A baseball doesn't change its shape when you throw it.

You can change the shape of a solid, but it takes energy. You could put a dent in your bike by hitting it with a hammer. You could tear the petals off a flower or break a dish by dropping it on the floor. You can burn wood or carve stone or cut paper. Changing the shape of a solid takes effort.

Look around. How many solids can you see? What shapes do they have?

You have to hit a bike hard to dent it.

It takes fire's energy to burn wood.

A sculptor using a chisel to carve marble

☁ *Water has no shape as it squirts from a hose.*

Liquids

You see many kinds of liquids every day. Water is a liquid, and so is milk. Honey, hot cocoa, and shampoo are all liquids. A liquid can be hot or cold. It can be thick and gooey or thin and runny.

All liquids are alike in some

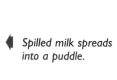

Spilled milk spreads into a puddle.

Honey is a gooey liquid. ▶

important ways. They feel wet, and they can be poured. And liquids have no shape of their own. They take on the shape of the **container** they are in.

Water takes on a tall, thin shape in a drinking glass. Water has a deep, round shape when it is in a fishbowl.

If you spill water on the floor, it spreads out and forms a puddle. Without a container to hold it, a liquid has no shape.

Water has a round shape in a fishbowl.

Liquids can be poured.

Gases

Gases are like liquids. They do not have a shape of their own. Gases just sort of float around. They spread out to fill whatever space there is. Usually, we can't see, or feel, or even smell gases. So how do you know gases are there?

Air is a gas, and you know it is all around you. You can feel it on your

These bright signs are actually tubes filled with neon gas.

You can see air when it fills out the sails of a boat on a windy day. ▶

cheek on a windy day. You can see it blow leaves across the yard. Without air, people and animals could not breathe. Without air, plants could not grow.

To see how air takes up space, try this experiment. Take a big breath. Can you see and feel how your chest moves out? Inside your body, your lungs are filling with air. The air is pushing your chest way out.

Now let out all that air. Do you see how your chest goes back to normal? When you breathe in and out, you are moving air. You cannot see this air, but you can tell how much space it takes up in your lungs.

You can see and feel the air in your lungs when you take a deep breath. ▶

Since helium is lighter than air, helium balloons float away when you let go of them.

Filling a balloon with helium gas

You can also see how gases take up space by looking at a balloon. The more air you blow into a balloon, the bigger it gets. Sometimes people use a gas called **helium** to fill balloons. Helium is lighter than air, so helium balloons float in air.

Here's another experiment. Put a straw in a glass of water, and blow into the straw. Do you see bubbles? You are blowing a gas called **carbon dioxide** into the water.

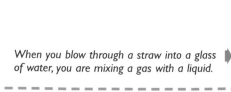

When you blow through a straw into a glass of water, you are mixing a gas with a liquid.

Changing Matter

Have you ever seen a solid change into a liquid? Have you ever seen a liquid change into a gas? Think about water.

When you pour water into a pot, it is a liquid. It is wet, it pours, and it has no shape of its own. If you put the pot of water into the freezer, what happens? When the water cools down, it freezes and becomes ice. Ice is a solid. It holds its own shape.

If you put the pot of water onto the stove and heat it, the ice will change back into a liquid. If you keep heating the water, it will begin to boil.

Water comes out of a faucet as a liquid. ▶

As liquid water boils, it changes into a gas called **steam**. Steam is invisible.

You can't see steam as it spreads out into the air. But you can do an experiment that will tell you how far the steam has spread. Ask an adult to help you add some cooking spices to boiling water. When the water turns into steam, it will smell like those spices. How far away can you stand

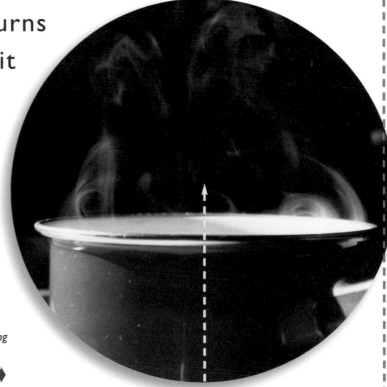

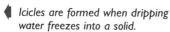
Icicles are formed when dripping water freezes into a solid.

Boiling water turns into a gas called steam.

and still smell the spices? That's how far the steam has spread.

Water is not the only material that can change from a solid to a liquid and from a liquid to a gas. Any solid will change into a liquid if it gets hot enough. The liquid will change back into a solid when it cools down. Any liquid will change into a gas if it gets hot enough. The gas will change back into a liquid when it cools down.

*Butter changes from a solid ▶
to a liquid when it melts.*

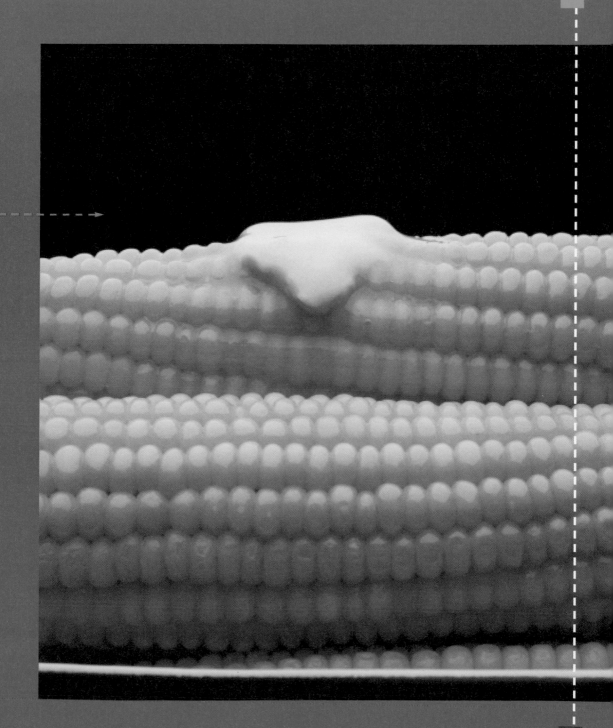

Matter, Wonderful Matter

Everything in the world is made up of matter—including you. Your hair, skin, teeth, and bones are solids. Your blood, sweat, and tears are liquids. The air you breathe into your lungs (and some-times burp out) is a gas. You are a perfect collection of solids, liquids, and gases!

Your tears are liquid.

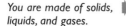
You are made of solids, liquids, and gases.

Glossary

carbon dioxide—the gas that you breathe out

container—an object that holds something

gases—a substance that can flow. Gas takes on the shape of the container it is in. Most gases are invisible.

helium—a gas that is lighter than air and is sometimes used to fill balloons

liquid—a substance you can pour. Liquids feel wet, can flow, and take on the shape of the container they are in.

matter—anything that takes up space. Everything you can see is made up of matter.

solids—materials that have their own shape and are usually hard

steam—the gas on vapor that is formed when water boils.

Did You Know?

- About 10 percent of Earth's surface is covered with ice. About 70 percent of Earth's surface is covered with ocean water.

- The bright light you see in a neon sign is a gas.

- Ice floats in liquid water because ice is less dense than water.

Want to Know More?

At the Library

Fowler, Allan. *Solid, Liquid, or Gas?* Chicago: Childrens Press, 1995.

Mebane, Robert C. *Air and Other Gases.* New York: Twenty-First Century Books, 1995.

Osbourne, Louise. *Solids, Liquids, and Gases.* Buffalo, N.Y.: Kids Can Press, 1997.

On the Web

How Things Work

http://rabi.phys.virginia.edu/HTW/

For information about why steam is invisible and ice cream melts

The Water Cycle

http://viking.nasm.edu/k12/pilot/water_cycle/grabber2.html

For activities and information about the water cycle

Through the Mail

Soil and Water Conservation Society

7515 N.E. Ankeny Road

Ankeny, IA 50021

For information about soil and water management and the environment

On the Road

Museum of Science

Science Park

Boston, MA 02114-1099

617/723-2500

To check out exhibits that explore many areas of science

Index

About the Author

Charnan Simon began her publishing career in the children's book division of Little, Brown and Company. She also served as an editor at *Cricket* magazine for six years and is now a contributing editor for *Click* magazine. Charnan Simon has written more than forty children's books. *Jane Addams: Pioneer Social Worker* won the NCSS Notable Trade Book in Social Studies in 1997. She lives in Madison, Wisconsin.